ISRAEL
the culture

Debbie Smith

A Bobbie Kalman Book

The Lands, Peoples, and Cultures Series

 Crabtree Publishing Company
www.crabtreebooks.com

The Lands, Peoples, and Cultures Series
Created by Bobbie Kalman

Coordinating editor
Ellen Rodger
Proofreader: Adrianna Morganelli

Project development, writing, editing, and design
First Folio Resource Group, Inc.
  Pauline Beggs
  Tom Dart
  Marlene Elliott
  Kathryn Lane
  Debbie Smith

Revisions and updates
Plan B Book Packagers
Redbud Editorial

Special thanks to
Shawky J. Fahel, J. G. Group of Companies; David H. Goldberg, Ph.D., Canada-Israel Committee; Steven Katari; Taali Lester, Israel Government Tourist Office; Alisa Siegel and Irit Waidergorn, Consulate General of Israel; Khaleel Mohammed

Photographs
Photo Researchers, Steven Allan: p. 9 (top), p. 20 (top), p. 23 (top), p. 29 (top), p. 30 (both); David Bartruff/Corbis: p. 11 (top); Pavel Bernshtam/Shutterstock, Inc.: p. 10 (top), p. 25 (top); Vitaliy Berkovych/Shutterstock, Inc.: p. 16 (top); Aron Brand/Shutterstock, Inc.: p. 7 (top); Natalia Bratslavsky/Shutterstock, Inc.: p. 11 (bottom); Corky Buczyk/Shutterstock, Inc.: p. 22 (bottom); discodave2000/Shutterstock, Inc.: p. 16 (bottom); Eyalos/Shutterstock, Inc.: p. 26; Bryan Firestone/Shutterstock, Inc.: p. 24 (bottom); Joel Fishman/Photo Researchers: p. 17 (bottom); Gordon Gahan/Photo Researchers: p. 23 (bottom right); Rostislav Glinsky/Shutterstock, Inc.: p. 27 (bottom); Louis Goldman/Photo Researchers: p. 23 (left); Annie Griffiths Belt/Corbis: p, 18 (bottom), p. 19 (top); Boris Katsman/Shutterstock, Inc.: p. 31 (bottom); David Lees/Corbis: p. 21 (top); Mikhail Levit/Shutterstock, Inc.: p. 11 (bottom); Nir Levy/Shutterstock, Inc.: p. 28; Tony Mathews/Shutterstock, Inc.: p. 12 (bottom); Yasha Mazur/Photo Researchers: p. 7 (bottom); David Mckee/Shutterstock, Inc.: p. 30 (top); Eoghan McNally/Shutterstock, Inc.: p. 27 (bottom); Richard T. Nowitz: p. 3, p. 4 (top), 5–6 (all), p. 8 (both), p. 9 (bottom), p. 10, p. 14 (bottom), p. 18 (top), p. 22 (both), p. 29 (right); pavelr/Shutterstock, Inc.: p. 15 (top); Losevsky Pavel/Shutterstock, Inc.: p. 12 (top); Glenda M. Powers/Shutterstock, Inc.: p. 20 (bottom); Richard T. Nowitz/Photo Researchers: p. 21 (bottom); Lily Rosen - Zohar/Shutterstock, Inc.: p. 4 (bottom); salamanderman/Shutterstock, Inc.: p. 1, p. 25 (bottom), p. 27 (top), p. 31 (top); Howard Sandler/Shutterstock, Inc.: p. 13, p. 14 (top); Elisei Shafer/Shutterstock, Inc.: p. 31 (middle); Eitan Simanor/Bruce Coleman: cover; Ted Spiegel/Corbis: p. 19 (right); Rob Swanson/Shutterstock, Inc.: p. 24 (top); Albert H. Teich/Shutterstock, Inc.: p. 30 (bottom); Ewa Walicka/Shutterstock, Inc.: p. 17 (top); Lisa F. Young/Shutterstock, Inc.: p. 15 (bottom)

Illustrations
William Kimber. The back cover shows an ibex, a wild goat native to Israel. An oud, a Middle Eastern instrument similar to a lute, appears at the head of each section.

Cover:
Israel is home to many faiths. This view of the Western Wall of old Jerusalem includes the Wailing Wall, a Jewish holy site, and the Dome of the Rock, a Muslim holy site.

Title page:
An Israeli store displays dozens of *kippot*, the small caps traditionally worn by observant Jewish men.

Library and Archives Canada Cataloguing in Publication

Smith, Debbie, 1962 Nov. 17-
    Israel : the culture / Debbie Smith.

(Lands, peoples, and cultures series)
Includes index.
ISBN 978-0-7787-9313-7 (bound).--ISBN 978-0-7787-9681-7 (pbk.)

    1. Israel--Civilization--Juvenile literature. 2. Israel--Social life and customs--Juvenile literature. I. Title. II. Series.

DS112.S64 2007   j956.94   C2007-906202-4

Library of Congress Cataloging-in-Publication Data

Smith, Debbie, 1962-
    Israel. The culture / Debbie Smith.
        p. cm. -- (The lands, peoples, and cultures series)
    "A Bobbie Kalman Book."
    Includes index.
    ISBN-13: 978-0-7787-9313-7 (rlb)
    ISBN-10: 0-7787-9313-3 (rlb)
    ISBN-13: 978-0-7787-9681-7 (pb)
    ISBN-10: 0-7787-9681-7 (pb)
    1. Israel--Civilization--Juvenile literature. 2. Israel--Religion--Juvenile literature. I. Title. II. Series.

DS112.S64 2007
956.94--dc22   2007041476

Crabtree Publishing Company

www.crabtreebooks.com   1-800-387-7650

Published in Canada
Crabtree Publishing
616 Welland Ave.
St. Catharines, ON
L2M 5V6

Published in the United States
Crabtree Publishing
PMB16A
350 Fifth Ave., Suite 3308
New York, NY 10118

Published in the United Kingdom
Crabtree Publishing
White Cross Mills
High Town, Lancaster
LA1 4XS

Published in Australia
Crabtree Publishing
386 Mt. Alexander Rd.
Ascot Vale (Melbourne)
VIC 3032

Contents

Israel is home to people of many **faiths**. Jews, Muslims, Druze, Christians, and Baha'is all live in this small country. Their religions guide their beliefs, influence their ways of life, and inspire their **cultures**. The art, music, dance, literature, and clothing of Israel all reflect religious faith in some way.

Israel is a meeting place of the old and new, of eastern and western. People wearing jeans and T-shirts shop beside others wearing **traditional** clothing. One radio station plays folk songs, while another plays rock-and-roll. An Israeli movie is featured on one theater screen, while a North American movie is featured on the screen right next to it.

(above) A Muslim woman holds out her hands in prayer.

(below) The Torah is the most important document of Judaism.

Israel is still a young country. As it grows older, the challenge for all of its people will be to develop their own identities while respecting the cultures and religions of those around them.

(opposite) A Christian monk wanders through the desolate Judean Desert.

To understand the people of Israel, it is important to understand a bit about their faiths or beliefs. About 76 percent of Israel's population is Jewish. About sixteen percent are Muslims. Christians, Druze, Baha'is, and many smaller religious groups make up the rest of the population. Some of these religions have common roots and share some of the same beliefs, such as the belief in one God. It is the differences between the religions, however, that make each truly interesting.

Judaism

Judaism is over 4,000 years old. Its teachings are partly based on ten commandments that God gave the Jewish people thousands of years ago. The most important teaching is that there is only one God. The Golden Rule, "Do unto others as you would have others do unto you," comes from the ten commandments.

The ten commandments are found in the Torah, the first five books of the Bible. This holy book includes other laws of Judaism and tells about the early history of the Jewish people.

(above) A young woman chants prayers from her siddur, the Jewish prayer book.

(below) Torah scrolls are handwritten by scribes who write on parchment using a feather pen and ink from an ancient recipe. It can take one year to write a Torah. Every letter and every space must be just right. A proofreader checks for errors.

(left) An Ethiopian Jew prays at the Western Wall. Around him slips of paper have been tucked into the crevices of the wall. On each of these papers is someone's prayer to God.

Branches of Judaism

At one time, most Jews were Orthodox. That means that they followed all the traditional laws and customs of their religion. Over time, some Jews abandoned many of the old ways and began living less Orthodox lives. Today, there are different branches of Judaism, including Orthodox, Conservative, Reform, and Reconstructionist. Each group still believes that there is only one God, but they practice their religion differently. For example, Orthodox Jews keep *kosher*, which means that they follow special dietary laws. They do not eat shellfish or pork, they do not eat milk and meat together, and they prepare their food in special ways. People who are less religious are not as strict in keeping these rules.

(below) As is the custom among ultra-Orthodox Jews, this three-year-old boy has waited until the holiday of Lag Ba'Omer to have his hair cut for the first time.

Islam

Islam is a religion that teaches peace, mercy, and forgiveness. People who practice Islam are called Muslims. They follow the teachings of the **prophet** Muhammad, who was born in 570 A.D., in the city of Mecca, Saudi Arabia. According to Islamic belief, Muhammad received the teachings of God, who Muslims call Allah, through the angel Jibril, or Gabriel. As Muhammad taught Allah's messages to others, Islam spread throughout the world. Today, there are two main sects of Islam: Sunni and Shiite. Most Muslims in Israel are Sunni.

(above) A family painted the doorway of their home to let neighbors know that they completed the **hajj,** *the pilgrimage to Mecca.*

(below) Muslims use special movements as they pray, including bowing and pressing their heads to their prayer mats.

The Five Pillars of Islam

Allah's instructions are recorded in the Qur'an, a holy book that is read by Muslims all over the world. There are five main principles, called the Five Pillars of Islam. The first pillar is that Muslims must declare that there is no God but Allah and Muhammad is his prophet. They must pray five times a day facing the Ka'bah, the most important shrine in Mecca. They are required to give charity to those in need and to fast in the daylight hours during the holy month of Ramadan. The fifth pillar of Islam is to perform the *hajj*, a **pilgrimage** to Mecca.

(left) Many groups of Christians live in Israel. They share some of the same beliefs, but each has its own customs and churches.

*(below) These Druze elders wear white turbans called **uqqals** that show they are among those who know their religion's secrets.*

Druze

The Druze religion is over 800 years old and has its roots in Islam. The Druze believe that Allah's teachings were revealed to a special group, including a messenger who came after the prophet Muhammad.

Little is known about the everyday religious practices of the Druze. Even in their own community, only a small group of people who have passed difficult tests know the secrets of their religion.

Christianity

Christianity began in Israel almost 2,000 years ago. It is based on the teachings of Jesus Christ. Jesus, a Jew born in the town of Bethlehem, in Israel, was believed to be God's son on Earth. He taught people to be good and righteous. Many people, however, did not agree with Jesus' teachings and he was **crucified**. Jesus' life and lessons are recorded in a holy book called the New Testament. The Christian Bible also contains the Old Testament, which tells of the time before Christ.

Baha'i

The Baha'i faith is based on the teachings of Baha'u'llah. Baha'u'llah was born in Tehran, Iran, in 1817, and died in Acre, known as Akko, Israel, in 1892. Baha'u'llah's followers believe that he was a prophet sent by God, just like Jesus and Muhammad. Baha'u'llah taught that all religions honor the same God, and that people of all ages, races, and sexes are equal. He also taught that God wants one world society where everyone accepts and respects each other.

 # Houses of worship

In Israel, people of all religions are free to pray in their own buildings. Jews pray in synagogues or temples, Muslims pray in mosques, and Christians pray in churches.

Mosques

Religious Muslims pray five times a day: before sunrise, in early afternoon, in late afternoon, after sunset, and before going to bed. Many Muslims pray in a mosque, which must be quiet and clean. Worshipers leave their shoes in a courtyard so they do not dirty their **holy** place. They also wash their hands, feet, and face before entering the mosque to pray. Traditional mosques have a tower, called a *ma'dhana* or minaret, from which a *muezzin*, or prayer caller, summons Muslims to prayer. A large dome covers the main prayer hall so that prayers can echo throughout the room. There is no furniture in this room. Instead, people worship on beautifully patterned rugs. A small alcove called a *mihrab* shows the direction of the Ka'bah. If the mosque is large enough, there is also a *minbar*, or platform, on which the leader of the service, the *imam*, stands.

(above) Torah scrolls stand behind the embroidered curtain of the Aron Hakodesh.

(top) The golden Dome of the Rock is framed by the top half of the Western Wall, the holy sites of two religions in Jerusalem.

Synagogues

Religious Jews pray three times a day: in the morning, afternoon, and evening. They usually pray at a synagogue, which is a place of worship, study, and celebration. Whether large or small, all synagogues have some features in common. The main room is an auditorium where people pray facing the holy Western Wall in Jerusalem. An *Aron Hakodesh*, or Holy Ark, holds the Torah scrolls. The *Ner Tamid*, or Everlasting Light, burns above the Ark. This light is a reminder that the light of the Torah will never die.

(above) An Armenian priest prays at the altar in the Church of the Nativity, in Bethlehem. This is the oldest Christian church in the world and is believed to be built on the site where Jesus was born.

*(above) Jews gather around an **Aron Hokodesh**, or **Holy Ark**, containing the Torah, during a ceremony at Jerusalem's Western Wall. The wall is the remains of an ancient temple.*

(right) The Shrine of the Báb, one of the holiest places of the Baha'i faith, was built in Haifa beginning in 1909. Its beautiful gardens make it a place for reflection and prayer.

11

A time to celebrate

(above) A Star of David outlined in celebration sparklers. The star is a symbol of Judaism and it appears on the Israeli flag.

(below) Food that is labeled **kosher** has been prepared and approved under Jewish dietary laws. This box contains food for a Passover celebration.

Hardly a month goes by in Israel when there is not some kind of holiday or festival. Jewish, Muslim, and Christian holidays all follow different calendars. The solar year is 365 days long or 366 days in a leap year. This is the time it takes for the earth to orbit around the sun. Christian holidays follow the solar calendar, where each new year begins on January 1 and ends on December 31.

Following the moon

The Muslim calendar is based on the lunar year. In the lunar calendar, each of the twelve months begins when a new moon appears. The lunar year is approximately eleven days shorter than the solar year. A Muslim holiday that falls in the winter one year may fall in the summer six or seven years later!

The lunar year, plus one month

The Jewish calendar is also based on the lunar year, but it adds an extra month seven out of every nineteen years. This way, holidays fall at about the same time every year. The Christian calendar divides time into two periods: before Jesus Christ was born (B.C.) and after he was born (A.D.). The Christian calendar entered its 21st century in the year 2000. The Muslim calendar begins in the year 622 A.D., the year Muhammad moved from Mecca to Medina to spread Allah's message. The Muslim calendar is now in its 15th century. The Jewish calendar is the oldest of the three calendars. It begins when Adam, who according to the Bible was the first human, was created by God. The Jewish calendar is now in its 58th century.

Jewish holidays celebrate the **harvest**, honor the heroics of legendary figures, and remember national and religious anniversaries. Here are some of the Jewish holidays.

Rosh Hashanah

Rosh Hashanah is the Jewish New Year. It falls in September or October. Rosh Hashanah is the first of ten days when people think about the mistakes they made over the past year and ask for forgiveness. During the holiday, they eat apples dipped in honey to symbolize their hope that the new year will be sweet. They also send New Year's cards to one another, wishing a happy, healthy, and sweet year.

Blowing the *shofar*

During Rosh Hashanah, Jews remember the story of Abraham and his son Isaac. According to the Torah, Abraham, the first Jew, was told to **sacrifice** Isaac to prove his faith in God.

When God realized that Abraham was ready to obey his command, he stopped Abraham and told him to sacrifice a ram instead. The *shofar* or ram's horn is blown on Rosh Hashanah to remind the Jewish people of Abraham's faith.

Yom Kippur

Yom Kippur, the Day of **Atonement**, falls ten days after Rosh Hashanah. On this holiest day of the year, people fast for 25 hours. By not drinking or eating anything, they ask forgiveness for the sins they committed in the past year. They also pray that God will inscribe their names for a good and healthy year in the "Book of Life."

*The **shofar**, or ram's horn, is blown on Rosh Hashanah, when Jews remember the story of Abraham and Isaac.*

Sukkot

Sukkot is a fall harvest festival. During this holiday, many families build *sukkot*, or huts, in their backyards. The sides are usually made of wood panels. The roof is made of long branches, with spaces left between them so that the sky can still be seen. Fruits and vegetables hang on the walls and from the ceiling.

During Sukkot, many families eat in their *sukkah*. Some even sleep there. The *sukkah* is a reminder of the huts that farmers used to live in at harvest time to be near their crops. It is also a reminder of the temporary shelters in which the Jewish people lived as they journeyed through the desert thousands of years ago.

(right) Each night of Chanukah, a candle is lit on the **menorah.**

Chanukah

Chanukah is a festival of lights that takes place in November or December. Two thousand years ago, the Syrian Greeks ruled Israel and would not allow the Jews to practice their religion. The Jews rebelled and recaptured their holy temple, which the Greeks had ruined. When the Jews went to relight the ever-burning *menorah*, they found just enough oil for one day. Then a miracle happened: the oil lasted for eight days until more oil could be brought to the temple. This is why Chanukah is celebrated for eight days.

(left) The **lulav** *and* **etrog** *are symbols of the harvest that are used in ceremonies during Sukkot. The* **lulav** *is made up of branches from the palm, willow, and myrtle trees. The* **etrog,** *which looks like a lemon, comes from a tree called the citron.*

Levivot

During Chanukah, Jewish people all over the world eat foods cooked in oil such as *soofganiyot*, which are doughnuts, and *levivot* or *latkes*, which are potato pancakes. *Levivot* are very easy to make! Here are the ingredients you will need:

6 potatoes, grated and drained

3 eggs, lightly mixed

1 medium onion, chopped

1 tsp (5 mL) salt

1/4 tsp (1 mL) pepper

1/4 cup (62.5 mL) flour

2 tsp (10 mL) oil

2 tsp (10 mL) baking powder

Mix all the ingredients together except the oil. Heat the oil in the frying pan. Form flat pancake shapes with the batter. Drop the *levivot* in the oil. Turn only once. Serve hot with sour cream or applesauce.

(above) Jews eat apples dipped in honey during Rosh Hashanah to make the new year sweet. Hamen's ears are a Purim treat.

(below) **Levivot,** *or potato* **latkes,** *are very tasty and easy to make.*

Purim

On Purim, families go to the synagogue to hear *Megillat Esther*, the Story of Esther. This story tells how the Jewish Queen Esther and her uncle Mordechai saved the Jews of Babylon by outsmarting Haman, the king's wicked advisor who wanted to kill the Jews. Every time people hear Haman's name, they make noise with noisemakers called *ra'ashanim* or *greggors*. They also eat special pastries called *hamantashen* or *oznei Haman*, which means Hamen's ears. These triangular-shaped pastries are filled with jam, nuts, poppy seeds, or prunes.

(below) **Ashkenazi** *lamb roast, or stuffed lamb, is a* **Pesach specialty in Israel.**

Pesach

Pesach, or Passover, celebrates the Jews' escape from slavery in Egypt. The holiday lasts for seven days in Israel and for eight days outside of Israel. Before Pesach, families clean their homes to get rid of every bit of leavened bread, which is bread that has yeast. In fact, in many parts of the country it is almost impossible to find bread in stores during Pesach! For the entire holiday people eat *matzah* instead. This unleavened bread is a reminder that the Jews left Egypt in such a hurry that they did not even have time to let their bread rise.

On Pesach, families gather for a special meal called a *seder*. During the *seder* they read the *hagaddah*, which tells the story of Pesach, and they eat special foods. Just before the meal is served, a piece of *matzah* is broken in half. This is called the *afikoman*. The leader of the *seder* hides one half of the *afikoman*. Then, at the end of the meal, children search for it in every corner of the home. The child who finds the *afikoman* gets a present.

(above) **A community Purim celebration in Netanya, Israel, where people dress as Esther and Mordechai.**

(above) Machine-made **matzah** bread is a plain, unleaven cracker bread. **Matzah** is eaten during Pesach to remind Jews of the Exodus from Egypt.

The Pesach *seder*

Each of these items plays a special part during this symbolic meal.

❶ This flat, unleavened bread is *matzah*.

❷ Drinking four glasses of wine, or grape juice for younger children, is part of the *seder* tradition.

❸ Families gather around the table to read the story of Pesach from the *hagaddah*.

❹ People dip *karpas*, or greens, in saltwater to remind them of the Jews' tears when they were slaves.

❺ A roasted egg reminds people of the destruction of the holy temple. Its shape is also a symbol of the continuity of life.

❻ People eat *marror*, or bitter herbs, as a reminder of the bitter lives that the Jews lived as slaves.

❼ The shankbone is a reminder of God's outstretched arm, which led the Jews out of Egypt.

❽ *Karpas* is a sign of spring, when Pesach is celebrated.

❾ *Charoset* is a mixture of apples, nuts, and wine or grape juice. It is a reminder of the mortar that the Jews used to build bricks in Egypt.

Muslim holidays

(above) During Ramadan, Muslims come to Jerusalem to pray at the Dome of the Rock.

Muslim holidays remember events that are described in the Qur'an and that took place during the life of the prophet Muhammad. The most important holidays are Id ul-Fitr and Id ul-Adha.

Ramadan

Ramadan is the ninth month of the Muslim calendar. It is considered a holy month because Muhammad first received Allah's messages during Ramadan. Adults and many older children spend Ramadan fasting from sunrise to sunset and praying. Fasting teaches them to value the good things that Allah has provided them and to remember the poor and the hungry. It also teaches **self-discipline**.

Id ul-Fitr

As soon as the new moon appears, Ramadan ends and the great celebration of Id ul-Fitr, the Festival of Fast-Breaking, begins. People prepare for the holiday by giving charity, called Zakat ul-Fitr. The money is used to buy food for Muslims who cannot afford it for the holiday. People celebrate Id ul-Fitr by praying at home and at the mosque. They visit relatives for a special meal in the middle of the day, often bringing cakes, dried fruits, and other gifts. In the middle of the night, children knock on doors in the neighborhood, beating on the *tabla*, a Middle Eastern drum, and singing "You who are asleep wake up and pray to Allah." In exchange, children are given sweets or money.

(left) After a day of fasting, a family sits down to a large, satisfying meal.

Id ul-Adha

Because Judaism and Islam have common roots, some holidays celebrate similar events. Id ul-Adha is the Festival of Sacrifice. This holiday recalls almost the same story as Rosh Hashanah, except in this version Abraham was asked to sacrifice his son Ishmael, not Isaac. When Abraham proved that he was prepared to obey Allah's command, he was told to sacrifice a lamb instead. On this holiday, Muslims go to the mosque in their finest clothes to pray. To remember the sacrifice, they kill a sheep, goat, or camel and share the meat with friends, relatives, and the poor.

(top) A family prepares sweets to take to a relative's house for Id ul-Fitr.

(right) Men pour out of a mosque during the holiday of Id ul-Fitr.

Christian holidays

The two most important Christian holidays are Christmas and Easter. They both mark important events in the life of Jesus Christ.

Christmas

Christmas marks the day that Jesus Christ was born. It is a feast day when families and friends get together, eat, and often exchange gifts. In Israel, pilgrims from all over the world gather around Manger Square in Bethlehem and listen to music from the Church of the Nativity. They also visit cities, such as Nazareth and Jerusalem, where Jesus spent part of his life. Like in other countries where Christmas is celebrated, families decorate their homes with Christmas trees. Children wait for the arrival of "Baba Noel," which is what Santa Claus is called in Israel.

(right) During Easter, Christians crowd the courtyard outside the Church of the Holy Sepulcher in Jerusalem.

(below) A reenactment of Christ's death.

Easter

Easter is the most important feast in the Christian calendar. During this time, Christians remember Jesus' death and resurrection. The holiday begins on Holy Thursday when Jesus had his last supper with his closest followers and continues until Easter Sunday when Jesus rose from the dead. Christians believe that Jesus died for the forgiveness of their sins and that his resurrection means they will be reborn in heaven.

During Easter, church bells ring and special services are held throughout the country. In some communities, special candles, known as Holy Lights, are lit outside churches after midnight mass and are passed from person to person.

A day of devotion

One day that Jews, Muslims, and Christians all celebrate is a day devoted to God or Allah. For Muslims this day is Friday, for Jews it is Saturday, and for Christians it is Sunday.

Shabbat

Shabbat, or the Jewish Sabbath, begins a little before sunset on Friday night and ends after dark on Saturday night. Families prepare for *Shabbat* as if they were welcoming a queen, the *Shabbat* queen. They dress in their finest clothes and cook a delicious meal. Before they eat their meal, they light *Shabbat* candles, drink a glass of wine or grape juice, and eat a special loaf of bread called *challah* after saying blessings.

Because *Shabbat* is meant to be a day of rest, Orthodox Jews do not work on this day. They also do not drive, spend money, talk on the phone, or turn on electricity. Instead, they go to synagogue, take long walks, visit friends, and discuss the Torah portion that was read during morning services. Life in Israel can be fairly quiet on *Shabbat*, especially in Orthodox neighborhoods where stores are closed and buses do not run.

(top) **A muezzin** *summons Muslims to worship at the mosque on Friday with a call to prayer.*

(left) **This father is helping his daughter bake a braided** challah.

21

Clothes for play and prayer

People wear many different types of clothing in Israel. Most dress in present-day clothing such as jeans, T-shirts, shorts, running shoes, skirts, and business suits. Others wear the traditional clothing of their **ethnic** group or culture.

Clothes for praying

When religious Jewish men pray, they drape a *tallit*, or prayer shawl, around their shoulders. They also put on *tephillin* for the morning prayers. Each of these boxes has long black leather straps. One box is tied to the forehead, the other to the left arm facing the heart. *Tephillin* symbolize that a person's mind, heart, and body are to be used for good and not for evil. Religious men always wear a *kippa*, or skullcap, on their heads as a sign of modesty before God. Men who are less religious might only wear a *kippa* when they are praying or when they are at a Jewish celebration.

(below) Some Chassidic men wear long black socks and breeches.

Chassidic Jews

Chassidic (pronounced ha-si-dic) means "pious ones." *Chassidic* Jews are a group of ultra-Orthodox Jews who reject many modern ways. They believe strongly in modesty. When women marry, they shave their heads or keep their hair covered with a wig or scarf. The men have full beards, very short hair, and *peyot*, or side curls. They wear wide-brimmed black hats, long black coats, white shirts, and a *tallit katan*, or small prayer shawl.

(above) A Jewish boy wears the clothing of prayer. Inside the small black boxes of the tephillin is a prayer: "Hear, oh, Israel. The Lord our God. The Lord is one."

Muslim Arabs

Many Muslims follow careful religious rules when choosing what to wear. They dress simply and modestly, according to the Qur'an's instructions. Very **devout** women and girls must cover their bodies completely, except when they are at home with close family. Men and boys must cover themselves from the waist to the knees. Many people observe these rules by wearing clothes that are fashionable in the country where they live. Others wear more traditional clothing. Religious women might wear long black gowns over their clothes, scarves to cover their heads, veils to cover their faces, and gloves to cover their hands. Religious men might wear robes that comes down to their ankles or loose pants with a long shirt on top. This long, loose clothing also protects them from the sun and keeps them cool in the hot weather.

(above) One Arab man dresses in modern clothing while another wears traditional dress, with a **kaffiyeh.** *The* **kaffiyeh** *is folded in half, draped over the head, and held in place with a double ring of black rope, called an* **akkal.**

(above) On special occasions, Bedouin *women wear elaborate costumes. Metallic veils decorated with coins cover these women's faces.*

(left) A young Arab boy yanks at his mother's head scarf to attract her attention.

23

Art and architecture

Art in Israel is as varied as the people who live in the country. Each group of people has its own artistic specialty, whether it is making intricate jewelry, building elaborate mosques, or weaving rich tapestries. Yet the groups also learn from each other and influence one another's work.

Jewish art

Jewish art in Israel is a mix of styles and themes. Paintings and sculptures have traditionally been based on stories from the Torah, events in history, and people's love of the country. One subject that is often portrayed in Jewish art is the Holocaust, during which six million European Jews were killed by the Nazis. In the mid-1900s, artists in Israel were influenced by the style of the Bezalel Academy of Arts and Crafts. The Bezalel was founded in Jerusalem in 1906. Its goal was to create an original Jewish style of art that combined techniques from Europe and the Middle East.

(above) A mosaic lion sculpture combines glass and tile.

More recently, artists have begun to experiment with different techniques and are exploring topics, such as nature, relationships, and emotions, that have meaning to people no matter where they live.

Muslim art

Muslim art is full of intricate patterns and designs that wind together flowers, vines, stars, and interesting geometric shapes and lines. These designs, called arabesques, can be seen in elaborate mosaics, finely carved wooden doors, and richly colored rugs. Some of the best examples of Islamic art are found on Muslim buildings, especially mosques. Muslims believe that only Allah can create living things. Showing humans and animals in art, especially in the art of religious buildings, is discouraged. The Dome of the Rock, in Jerusalem, is considered the first Muslim masterpiece of art.

(left) An Israeli artist paints scenic landscapes in bright colors.

Calligraphy

Muslims believe the Qur'an to be Allah's exact words, so they spend a lot of time making this holy book look beautiful. They use calligraphy, or fine writing, and decorate the Qur'an with arabesques. Quotations from the Qur'an and Muhammad's sayings, written in calligraphy, also decorate buildings, tiles, pottery, wood, and metalware.

Architecture old and new

Israel is home to some of the world's most well-known architectural wonders. The Western Wall in Jerusalem's old city, is a stone retaining wall from the Second Temple. Its massive slabs stood between 516 B.C and 70 A.D. The Dome of the Rock is a golden domed Muslim shrine built between 687 and 691 A.D. Its dome is surrounded by thousands of inlaid tiles.

(above) Israel has many ancient ruins that date from different empires and time periods.

In modern Israel, architecture varies in style from European-influenced houses with red tile roofs, built in the late 1800s, to 1960s public buildings that incorporate oriental or Islamic styles. Haifa-born Canadian architect Moshe Safdie, has designed buildings all over the world, including the Holocaust Museum at Yad Vashem, and the airport near Tel Aviv. His style, which emphasizes light and angles, has influenced architecture in Israel and throughout the world. New construction projects in Jerusalem have altered the look of the city, bringing more high rises and glass towers.

(left) A Tel Aviv apartment building with its decorative finishes, replicates the sculptural style of Spanish architect Antoni Gaudi.

25

Leisure time

Israel's major cities are vibrant places and Israelis have an appetite for life. The streets are alive with cafés, theaters, and restaurants. Although Hebrew and Arabic are the official languages, you can hear languages such as Yiddish, Russian, French, or Hungarian in the streets of Israel's cities.

Theater and music

Israel has many theater companies that perform in several languages, as well as an opera company and two major orchestras. Whether attending a concert, listening to the radio, or chanting prayers, music is an important part of life in Israel. Some music has its roots in the Bible or Qur'ran. Other music has more modern themes that are not based on religion. Hebrew folk songs, for example, express people's hope for permanent peace in a country that has fought many wars.

Music styles

In Israel's early days, public sing-alongs were encouraged as one way to build a nation. People sang folk songs about the land and the desire for peace and a strong country. Sing-alongs were especially popular in the *kibbutz*. Over time, Israeli music changed to incorporate the different styles and tastes of music brought by people from Europe and North Africa. Arab and Yeminite music brought new beats and sounds from instruments such as the *oud*, a string instrument, the *tabla*, a drum, and the *mizmar*, a powerful, bagpipe-sounding reed instrument. Modern Israeli rock, pop, and hip-hop music sometimes mix these traditional sounds.

Friends meet at a waterside café to talk about movies, music, and politics.

Dance

In Israel, ever since ancient times, dance has been a way to express joy. Foot-stomping, hand-clapping folk dances are a large part of many celebrations. The *debka* and the *hora* are still performed at weddings and celebrations. The *debka* is an Arab folk dance with many different steps. Some are performed only by men, some only by women, and others by both. The *debka* can be danced in a circle or a line. The *hora* is the most famous Jewish folk dance. The *hora* was first danced in Romania, but now it is danced at Jewish celebrations around the world, often in a circle.

How about some sport?

Israel's warm climate means people spend a lot of time outdoors enjoying the weather and playing sports. Soccer is a popular outdoor sport and basketball is a popular indoor sport. Israel has a professional soccer league with teams in several cities and a basketball league that recruits players from the United States and other countries. Israelis are avid fans and follow their teams throughout the season.

(top) Bird watching is an activity that requires good eyesight and a lot of patience!

(middle) Israel's Saban Klemi skillfully evades Ireland's Ian Harte in a 2004 World Cup soccer match in Ireland.

(right) A kitesurfer catches a wave on the Mediterranean. Extreme watersports are popular along the coast.

Language and communication

People in Israel love to read newspapers, especially the big weekend papers that are published on Fridays. They also enjoy watching the news on television and listening to hourly news broadcasts on the radio. This news-gathering habit started many years ago when Israel was at war with its neighbors and the people of the country needed to know if they were in danger. Israel is not at war today, but like people everywhere, Israelis still want to know what is happening in their country and around the world.

Soldiers from the Israeli Defence Force (IDF) patrol neighborhoods in some areas of the country. Communicating with people on the street and being aware of the world, is just one way to prevent terror attacks from happening.

On the radio

There is a lot more on the radio besides the news. People can listen to music, talk shows, traffic reports, and special children's programs in many different languages. There is even a station for people who have come to Israel from other countries. For example, **immigrants** from the former Soviet Union can listen to programs in Russian and people from Ethiopia can listen to programs in their language, Amharic.

Satellite radio has also brought radio programs to Israel from around the world. Satellite radio is a radio service sent by satellite to paying customers around the world. People buy special equipment and pay a monthly fee for the service. They can listen to over 100 radio stations without commercials. Israel Radio broadcasts news and features from Israel and about Israel to satellite radio listeners around the world.

(above) Satellites are popular for television viewing and computer internet services.

The TV guide

Until the 1990s, Israel had just one television channel and it was on the air for only seven hours a day. If your television had an antenna and you pointed the antenna in just the right direction, you might have been able to tune in to programs from neighboring countries such as Egypt, Jordan, Cyprus, or Lebanon. In 1993, Israel's second channel began broadcasting. Cable television came to most of the country a year later. Today, Israelis receive over 40 channels through cable and even more if they have satellite television. They watch programs from countries such as the United States, France, Germany, India, Italy, Morocco, Spain, Russia, and Turkey. Children in Israel are learning words from many different languages just by watching TV!

(right) Customers browse through piles of books during the annual Hebrew Book Week. Israelis are avid book readers and thousands of Hebrew and Arabic books are published each year.

29

Israel has endured many wars and conflicts since independence was declared in 1948. The War of Independence began the day after, when the country's Arab neighbors did not recognize Israel's right to exist and invaded. Fifteen months later, Israel emerged victorious. Through the decades, several other wars followed, and Israelis gained both more territory, and confidence in their ability to defend themselves. Israel built a strong defense force and an alliance with the United States to help ensure its survival.

Fight for territory

The War of Independence displaced thousands of Palestinians. They became refugees in other countries or stayed clustered in occupied territories that became part of Israel. The Six Day War, in 1967, gave Israel control of more territory such as Egypt's Sinai Desert, Syria's Golan Heights, and Palestinian areas including the Gaza Strip, the West Bank, and East Jerusalem.

(below) Two girls hold a banner declaring their support for Israel at a rally in Washington, D.C.

Land for peace

Other wars followed, but the end of the war did not mean peace and security for Israel. In 1979, Israel began returning land in return for recognition and peace. The Sinai was returned to Egypt in 1979. Beginning in the 1980s, Palestinian uprisings, or Intifadas, started in the occupied territories. Through the Palestinian Authority, Palestinians were given control over parts of the West Bank and Gaza Strip in 1993. Israel began withdrawing its troops from the Gaza Strip in 2005.

(above) A massive security wall now divides Israel from Palestinian West Bank territory.

Today, the final status of Palestine has yet to be determined. Removing its troops from Gaza was a difficult decision for Israel. Many **settlers** had built homes there and had to be dragged out by the Israeli Defence Force.

Building a wall

In their fight for an independent Palestine, some Palestinians have resorted to acts of terror. **Suicide bombings** have become more common in Israel over the last 15 years. The government of Israel began building a wall, or barrier, around the West Bank in 2002. It hopes the wall will decrease future attacks and end the violence. Critics of the wall say Palestinian land was **annexed** to build the wall and that it has not contributed to a permanent peace. Supporters say the wall has decreased suicide bombings inside Israel and has made Israelis feel safer. The search for lasting peace continues.

(above) Heavily guarded borders are a reality for Israel.

(below) A suicide bombing in an Israeli city tore apart this shop. Suicide bombings on buses and in public places have killed many people in Israel. Israel has responded to bombings and rocket attacks with strict security for Palestinians, and by launching raids and rockets against militants in Palestinian territories and other areas.

(left) Terrorists launched rocket attacks from Lebanon that destroyed buildings and killed people in Haifa, Israel, in 2006. Israel responded with air strikes in southern Lebanon.

31

Glossary

annex To incorporate or bring territory into an existing country, city, or area

atonement The act of asking for forgiveness for sins

Bedouin Arabic tribes who move from place to place in the desert in search of grazing land and water for their livestock

crucify To put to death by nailing to a cross

culture The customs, beliefs, and arts of a distinct group of people

devout Devoted to religion

ethnic Describing or relating to social groups connected by race, language, heritage, or religion

faith Religious beliefs

harvest The gathering of crops

holy Having special religious importance

immigrate To come to settle in a different country

monk A member of a male religious community who has taken certain vows, such as silence or poverty

pilgrimage A religious journey to a sacred place

prophet A person who is believed to speak on behalf of God

sacrifice To offer to a god

scribe A person who copies manuscripts and documents

self-discipline The ability to control one's feelings and actions

settlers Israeli Jews who settle or move to territory under Israel's control since the 1967 Six Day War

suicide bombers People who kill themselves while committing an act of terror

traditional Describing customs that are handed down from one generation to another

ultra-Orthodox Jew A Jewish person who closely follows the religion's ancient laws and traditions

Index